The Lord is my shepherd;
I shall not want.
He makes me to lie down
in green pastures;
He leads me beside the still waters.
He restores my soul;
He leads me in the paths of
righteousness for His name's sake.
Yea, though I walk through the
valley of the shadow of death,
I will fear no evil; For You are with me;
Your rod and Your staff,
they comfort me.
You prepare a table before me
in the presence of my enemies.
You anoint my head with oil;
My cup runs over.
Surely goodness and mercy
shall follow me all the days of my life;
and I will dwell in
the house of the Lord forever.

The LORD is my shepherd.

The Lord God made me and made everything around me. God loves me like a good shepherd loves his sheep.

I shall not want.

Sheep need a loving shepherd to take good care of them every day. He gives them every-thing they need.

He makes me to lie down in green pastures.

The shepherd finds grassy fields where his sheep can eat their fill. Then they rest and relax because He is with them.

He leads me
beside the still waters.

Every day the good shepherd
needs to find clean water and
quiet streams for his thirsty sheep.

He restores my soul.

Whenever a lamb is missing, the loving shepherd quickly searches everywhere until he finds it.

The shepherd is so happy he found his precious lamb. He gladly carries his lamb back home.

He leads me in the
paths of righteousness,
for His name's sake.

Shepherds know which trails lead to green mountain pastures. The sheep need to follow their shepherd on the right paths.

Yea, though I walk through
the valley of the shadow
of death, I will fear no evil;
For You are with me.

In times of trouble and danger, the good shepherd never leaves his sheep. If they keep their eyes on him, they feel calm and at peace.

Your rod and . . .

. . . Your staff, they comfort me

The shepherd uses his rod to protect his sheep. He uses his staff to lead them and to lovingly stroke their back.

You prepare a table before me in the presence of my enemies.

A shepherd constantly protects his sheep from their enemies—poisonous weeds, snakes and other wild animals.

You anoint my head with oil

During hot summers, pesky flies upset the sheep. But the sheep calm down when the shepherd pours special oil on their heads.

My cup runs over

In the evening, the shepherd gives his thirsty sheep plenty of cool water to drink. He lets them drink as much they want from the bowl.

Surely goodness and mercy will follow me all the days of my life.

The shepherd has taken good care of his sheep all summer. Now it is time to return home. He follows them down the mountain to make sure no one is left behind.

And I will dwell in the house of the Lord forever.

The shepherd brings his sheep home,
where they will live with him forever.
His home is full of joy, peace and LIFE.
It is a home of love—the perfect home.

A thousand years after David wrote Psalm 23, one of his descendants was born in David's home town of Bethlehem.

That special baby was named Jesus. He was God's Gift of Love to all people.

When Jesus grew up, He said:

"I am the good shepherd
and I know My sheep...
I lay down My life for the sheep.

"My sheep hear My voice and
I know them, and they follow Me.
And I give...them eternal life,
and they shall never perish;
neither shall anyone snatch them
out of My hand."

John 10:14-15, 27-28

Once Jesus told a story of a shep-herd who had 100 sheep. When one sheep got lost, the shepherd searched everywhere until he finally found it.

He carried his precious sheep home and had a big celebration! He was so happy he had found his lost sheep.

Then Jesus said, *"I say to you, there is joy in the presence of the angels of God over one sinner who repents."* Luke 15:10

We all are like "lost sheep."
Jesus came to find us and to save us.
He suffered and died on a cross
for all the wrongs we've done.
His friends laid His body in a tomb.

Then God raised Jesus from the dead.
Jesus is alive! He is with us today!

Jesus wants to be your
Good Shepherd and your Savior.
He gave His life for you, and
He invites you to give your life to Him.

Dear Jesus,

Thank You for Your love! Forgive me for all the wrongs I've done. Thank You for dying on the cross for me. Now I give my life to You and I receive You as my Savior and my Good Shepherd.

*(sign)*____________________________

Now YOU are part of God's family.

You will live with God now and forever.

You have a whole new life!

- Love God. Love other people.
- Talk with God. Listen for God's voice.
- Read the Bible. Trust God each day.

"The LORD bless you and keep you;
The LORD make His face shine upon you,
and be gracious to you;
The LORD lift up His countenance
upon you, and give you peace."

Numbers 6:24-26

KIDS/CHD/FCT/PCP/CMS

Ages 6+

ISBN-13: 978-1-59317-466-8

90000

9 781593 174668

Warner Press Kids™

educate • nurture • inspire

www.warnerpress.org